Can I Divorce?

DR. CARLINA A. WILKES, D.MIN.

Library of Congress Cataloging-in-Publication Data has been applied for.

ISBNs: 978-1-957551-00-5 (paperback), 978-1-957551-01-2 (eBook)

Cover & Interior Design by: Bledsoe Publishing Company LLC

Published by: Bledsoe Publishing Company LLC

Printed in the United States of America

DEDICATION

To my dear beloved mother, who departed this life on December 22, 2020, your words to me will forever be in my heart. "Carlina, when are you going to get your doctorate?" I remember it as the day you spoke it to me, and I said, "Mom, I am done with school, and I don't think that is going to happen." Your very words were, "That is what you say, and we will see." I chuckle now that you spoke those prophetic words over my life more than seven or more years ago, and they have come to full fruition. You didn't get a chance to read this book; however, I am thanking GOD that you did know that I finished my education before you crossed over into eternity. I love you, Mom, forever.

Carlina

TABLE OF CONTENTS

ACKNOWLEDGEMENTS

It is with great pleasure to take this time to praise those who have supported me in the pursuit of my education and Ministry, MY FAMILY.

To my parents, I am sure that you did not understand what was in store for my life when you gave me the name that you did. You choose Carlina as my first name of German and Italian origins, meaning free man, free person, and select Annette for my middle name: French and Hebrew root, meaning grace, gracious, or He (GOD) has favored me. Both meanings describe my personality explicitly in my life. I am so thankful for my name, and I appreciate it. However, you gave me the name, and I now know that GOD had ordained it to be what it is for this appointed time.

To Thomas, my wonderful husband, a very reserved man who does not ask for much but has never interfered in my accomplishments and has supported me whole-heartedly. Sweetheart, I know that I have become the woman I am because of our relationship, I have grown to know GOD more excellently, and I thank you for that. No matter how many storms we have been through over the last forty years, I can say it was worth the journey. GOD has kept not only me but you as well.

To our four children, Matthew, Jermaine, E'Lisia, and MaKayla, you four have had to share me with family, U.S. Army, my job, my Ministry, and my time away from home. Whatever the reason, I am sure that you did not mind from time to time. However, for the most part, I know you would prefer for your mom to be plain and unpopular with others. I may not have given you all the riches that the world could offer; my goal was to pass on traits that could be an example that could carry on for generations to come.

To all my extended family, grandchildren, aunts, uncles, cousins, nieces, nephews, Godchildren, Godparents, spiritual parents, adopted family members, words cannot express my LOVE for you and anything you have done to support me.

To my close-knit friends and colleagues in the gospel down through the years, I am reserved not to call names for the sake of leaving Someone out. The list is too long to mention. What I will say is this, "my best friends know who they are," and I appreciate your support in every way. As for my colleagues and the Saints that have prayed and continue to pray for me, how could I ever repay you for your unselfish love and prayers that you have given to me.

– Thank You

ENDORSEMENTS

"I want to acknowledge my support for Mrs. Carlina Wilkes and the book she has written, "Can I Divorce." Carlina has striven hard and has been blessed to overcome many obstacles to further her education, support her family, and fulfill her vision through written expression. I salute Carlina for her accomplishments and pray for her new endeavors as GOD moves her forward in Ministry." – Bishop Charles M. Finnell, Pastor, Christ Temple Apostolic Faith Assembly

"One of the greatest gifts we can give to each other is the gift of knowing we are not alone. Through Carlina's transparency and openness, she has willingly shared her story of challenges and triumphs in her marriage with me. Need encouragement? Need hope? Need to know that you are not alone? Talk to my dear Sister Carlina. She has indeed been a blessing to my life." – Tonya Patterson

"I can't think of a better person to write on such a massive subject of Divorce than Dr. Carlina A. Wilkes. Many of us…I'm included, dare not touch a topic because we have experienced it.

GOD tells us about marriage in Genesis 2 and talks about cleave. When you think of the word cleave…the author, Dr. Wilkes, is our example. Like glue, she has kept her marriage intact. Thank you, Dr. Wilkes, for sharing with us your heartfelt love for GOD standard that we are to remain married unto death do us part, or until we go up in the rapture." – Evangelist Shirley Jean Smith *"Everyone, married or not married, has something to look forward to in reading "Can I Divorce?" by Carlina A. Wilkes,*

D.Min. Regardless of current marital status, let's admit that we have all had questions about the topic of marriage and divorce. Most pulpits and biblical commentaries will present only one side of marriage – the impenetrable perfection of matrimony in which two people are equally yoked in spiritual harmony. Make no mistake, this book fully supports the sanctity and sacredness of marriage and does not offer excuses for breaking marital vows. So, what is different about "Can I Divorce?". Unlike any other author, Dr. Wilkes has done a tremendous job of providing sound biblical analysis for those who have fallen short of perfection.

I am both a family law attorney and a church advisor. I have seen marriage and divorce from all spectrums – from the perfect to the broken, from the wayward to the spiritual. So, believe me when I say that I am impressed with Dr. Wilkes' insight and perspective. Dr. Wilkes has been married to the same person for four decades, yet her willingness to be transparent and inspirational for the good of the body of Christ is commendable. "Can I Divorce?" is a must-read.

Direct, instructional, and enlightening, "Can I Divorce?" exposes the religious misinterpretations and unsubstantiated claims crippling many people today. It offers grace with the chapter on "GOD's Perspective" clearly and concisely. This is a must-read for anyone who seeks a better understanding of the institution of marriage and how to minister to those who have survived a divorce." – Sylvia Brown, J.D. Attorney

A PERSONAL MESSAGE

Dear Reader,

What a challenge this has been to get this publication completed. Never in my lifetime did I imagine that I would pursue a doctorate or write a book; this was not on a bucket list or a personal goal; nevertheless, here it is.

Let me take this time to encourage you that whatever your struggles have been in your life, or you may be going through even now, it is not for naught. Trust me when I tell you that GOD wants to use you for a testimony to help someone be delivered or encouraged through their woes, test, and trials. Become transparent, write the story, and watch GOD get the GLORY!!

Allow the manifestation of his power to flow from your mind to pages as it produces an outcome of revival to save a soul. Don't allow shame, fear, or the deep dark secrets to be a tool for the enemy to keep you from achieving a brighter future.

RELEASE to the PRESS because someone is waiting on you to throw out that lifeline for survival. I pray that you too will be the next best seller on the market and that I will read your work soon.

Sincerely,

Dr. Carlina A. Wilkes

FOREWORD

It gives me great honor to write this forward on Dr. Carlina A. Wilkes's book, "Can I Divorce." This book will provide help to a lot of people who have had a mindset of misunderstanding Divorce. Many lives will be changed, as there will be a great move of GOD, and individuals will understand that they are divorcing a body and not GOD.

This book, "Can I Divorce," is not only appropriate for those going through a divorce but difficult situations in life as well. We all face challenging moments in life, and this book serves as a source of inspiration and guidance. Dr. Carlina A. Wilkes, I know, drew inspiration from GOD and shows the direction of strengthening one's faith in the LORD.

In conclusion, this book is a must-read for all individuals who would like to experience divine intervention in their lives.

God Bless You,
Dr. Laron Matthews, PhD
Prophet, Teacher and Pastor
Restoration Foundation Prophetic International Ministry
Harvey, Illinois

AUTHOR OF: *Love: The Unfinished Chapter* and *The Encounter with Wisdom: The Secrets of Her*

PREFACE

Can you imagine being a 21-year-old newlywed with less than three years of marriage and being told that you would be a marriage counselor? Strange as it sounds, in 1983, a clear, crisp voice spoke those very words as I was getting out of a car in Baumholder, West Germany. How frightening this was to me that GOD was speaking in such a manner! No formal warnings, a babe in Christ, and I was pregnant with my third child. I am sure that I thought it was hormones causing me to hallucinate. Whatever the case, the prophetic word had been spoken and ordained to happen. In 2003 the activation of that call came to pass. It was during a troubling time in my marriage. GOD revealed the hidden mysteries found in His Holy word concerning marriage and divorce to me.

The Holy Spirit provided me with answers to questions that I had asked in my heart concerning certain scriptures and the absolute truth behind such a mysterious topic. I needed to know the truth. I saw that it was happening way too often, especially in Christendom. Marriages in our society casually are treated as shoes – off with the old and on with the new. I heard an individual say, "I will keep on doing it till I get the right one."

Marriage is as sacred as GOD himself. No one seemed to relate to the importance of the unity of the marriage covenant or even expound upon the alternatives to explore when it gets rough in a marriage. Instead, divorce always seems to be the first option. Hopefully, this information will explain GOD's grounds for divorce to believers other than the same old traditional repetitive teachings. There is a lack of knowledge, and it is time for us to realign our thinking with the scriptures.

People often say, "GOD never makes a mistake, or He puts no more on us than we can bear." Those words sound so innocent and straightforward until things begin to happen unexpectedly or are uncomfortable in their lives. We even have the nerve to get upset and mummer these words, "woo is me," or "why me," becomes a free ticket to suffer anything. If GOD said it, that settles it. We certainly know that His ways are not our ways, and whatsoever He wants out of us, is bound by "Let there be." This information is intended to be a tool for those facing divorce or separation. I gained this knowledge through my journey of many tears, sleepless nights, fasting, and prayer with the hope that, and from my experience, other marriages can be saved.

I hope this book (not replacing the Bible) but to serve as a GOD-given manual to men and women struggling with one of the most controversial subjects in Christendom, DIVORCE/SEPARATION. If you are genuinely searching for Biblical truths and answers, this is a tool to help. The pages of this book will bring peace and comfort that will help you navigate your storm—and experience an outcome of Peace, Hope, Love, and good communication in the years to come.

This book will provide some insight into many familiar scriptures and some new understanding and clarity. Some scholarly literary views will also help support the revelation that GOD wants his people to know and not perish because of the lack of knowledge. The author's opinion is that each reader will prayerfully keep an open mind of the content they are about to read. It is easy to challenge new information that is unknown as general knowledge; however, with courage, [someone] who reads this book's contents will receive revelation in the same way GOD gave it to me.

Also, I would like to testify how the ALMIGHTY GOD is a keeper as I was awakened in the wee hours of the morning. GOD was guiding my mind, body, and spirit through the storm of life. Again, I cannot stress enough how I would never have made it without fasting, praying, and the leading of the Holy Spirit. He kept me when I felt hopeless, depressed, oppressed, suicidal, not to mention losing my mind.

Lastly, my heart continuously rejoices, as GOD has brought me through and continues to keep me now for forty years and counting in my marriage. I wanted to give up, walk away, and eliminate the pain many days, but thanks be to GOD, which unveiled the strongholds and faults, purging my insecurities and redirecting my love as he helped me not give up on my wonderful husband. Now, I can say that life is grand! I endured through it all! Every day gets sweeter and sweeter – both naturally and spiritually.

Adhering to the words of Acts 14:17, ... *Nevertheless, he left not himself without witness...* and now I have become one of those witnesses who can testify, that you can do it too! Hopefully, your future testimony of obedience to the written WORD OF GOD and waiting on him will help others achieve what will and can be possible if they KEEP trusting and believing that GOD WILL DELIVER!!

Please keep in mind, even if you have already divorced and your testimony may be of other circumstances, do not feel guilty or allow the enemy to convict you for something you did not know after reading this book. Talk to our HEAVENLY FATHER and let him be the driving force that will give you complete assurance concerning the issue of divorce. GOD and GOD alone will have the final judgment according to His Word. Rest in the LORD and let his peace give you the solace needed for what has already transpired.

INTRODUCTION

Today in our society, divorce statistics have increased so drastically until it has become out of control, even in Christendom. It seems that no one wants to compromise and find solutions to what appears to be a continual problem in marriages or apply the proper application by using what GOD intended marriage to be.

Believers, despite the norm, we are not to follow the traditions of our society. We must realize that the unchurched or those who marry without understanding may never know what marriage was intended to be and only feel that they are to settle their irreconcilable differences with divorce. For us, this is not our plight unless it is the grounds GOD has stated in his word. As Believers, we are to be the example for those in our society, and if we are practicing rudiments and traditions, how can we expect them to see GOD's design for marriage? It is troubling when supposedly two individuals [man and a woman] who say that they are spirit-filled, Born Again Believer "CANNOT" resolve their problems when they both profess the hope in the one who is the problem solver.

Does not the scripture declare in Philippians 4:13, "*I can do all things through Christ, which strengtheneth me?*" Does not the Bible say unto us that we are our brother's keeper? Does it not tell us that we are helpers one to another? Whatever happened to if we bring our gift to the altar, and if we remember that we have an ought against our brethren, we should leave our gift and go our way and be first reconciled to thy brother and then come and offer up our gift? Let us not forget that the Bible says we are to forgive seven times seventy, in "ONE DAY!"

These are questions and facts that should press a firm conviction into married couples' hearts, as these and many other passages relate to salvation and marriage. Could it be possible that this is the root of many issues or that someone did not seek out all the scriptures and its promises? Or is it that individuals sought their agendas rather than GOD's? There is a purpose why GOD intends for his people to understand and apply practical principles to our daily lives. Providing such an understanding and application will allow us to live in peace and harmony with others and within ourselves. Firmly this conviction in which I believe was the sole purpose of the Ten Commandments, GOD delivering a message that holds many of the secrets for humanity as a whole and certainly a solid foundation to be used within the arena of marriage. Two of which we will discuss later in one of the chapters.

Again, please keep in mind as you read the information within this book's pages, I caution you as a reader that it may conflict with teachings you have received in the four-walls housing the congregation [aka...The Church]. Some of which will challenge your mind to question past doctoral instructions and practices resulting from misinterpreted, misquoted scriptures or manipulating control of many congregants. Please realize that it is okay for you to disagree; however, take the time to carefully study the scripture. Allow the Holy Spirit to help you rightly divide the word of truth, and have an open mind for understanding to become transparent concerning this subject DIVORCE. Then give an honest verdict accordingly with this new evidence on what GOD has to say about "Divorce."

Can I Divorce?

Every way of a man is right in his own eyes; but the LORD pondereth the hearts. Proverbs 21:2

Knowing the truth of the matter is what GOD wants from us and not inventing ways to change his practices.

– Dr. Carlina A. Wilkes

CHAPTER ONE

Defining Divorce and Its History

All words have origins and meanings, which causes ideas to be expressed and portray a picture to the user and receiver communicated either by written or verbal form. Generally, a person engages in conversation with other individuals in an attempt to understand their thoughts clearly. The bible beautifully describes this outline for us in the words of Proverbs 4:7, *Getting wisdom is the wisest thing you can do! And whatever else you do, develop good judgment.* (NLT)

Bringing us to this point why it is necessary to know more about the subject, divorce, and the likes thereof. As we answer the initial question, we will build a foundation for its meaning. Yes, it is common knowledge that there is a spiritual application confined in the context of the Holy Bible; however, other resources will be a reference to help better understand this complex subject. Building from the following sources, such as: (1) a historical outline, cited by a legal professional's perspective, (2) methodology of terms quoted from Merriam-Webster's dictionary, and (3) the biblical truth, the ultimate law behind it all.

So, what is Divorce? Who is to blame? Can it ever be overcome? Some say yes, and some say no. Some have pros and cons to their perception of the subject. Whatever is the view of the matter, the sting of divorce is never elegant. Our society casually promotes divorce as if it is insurmountable. Many marriages suffer and are intense with complex situations that bring challenging issues and underline forces to the courtroom of life. Challenges that exhibit resentful emotions and behaviors, allowing other outside sources to take precedence over logical thinking, without considering a definitive response for a positive outcome, other than divorce.

Yes, this dark, evil topic has caused many lives to be destroyed, leaving many unanswered questions about why it happens that will provoke honest answers to this subject. Whenever the phrase divorce emerges, it is common knowledge that it is because of an ended marriage. The truth of the matter is, how valid were the grounds for the marriage to end in divorce? Later in chapter four: GOD's Perception and Ground Rules, we will discuss the biblical legal grounds.

Understand that the subject of divorce cannot be discussed without connecting it to marriage. Marriage is a serious matter and not handled as a bag of groceries or a competition. Marriage is not a contract as described in the dictionary: "a written or spoken agreement, especially one concerning employment, sales or tenancy, that is intended to be enforceable by law." Rather a commitment of an institution bound for life, regulated by an oath stemming from the WORD OF GOD. Supported by the recording of 1 Corinthians 7: 10-11, *"To the married I give you this command (not I but the Lord): A wife must not separate from her husband. But if she does, she must remain unmarried or else be reconciled to her husband. And the husband must not divorce his wife."* (NIV) A more in-depth explanation will be provided further as well in chapter four.

Such a passage is one of many scriptures that testifies what God intended from the beginning of time. On the other hand, many teachers, preachers, and individuals have taken such passages without further researching the full content of what was documented in the text to understand fully. GOD's word is precise that he never intended for a man and a woman to be apart once they committed to one another. GOD wanted unification as this relates to his desire for humanity to be one with him. There is something unique and mysterious about GOD's oneness, and at the same time, it firmly relates to him and our relationship with each other.

It is a fact that with man, one plus one equals two; however, with GOD, one plus or times himself always equals whatever he wants it to be, and frankly, it is "ONE" coordinated through unification, and not division. How so? The Apostle Paul gives us a glimpse of this insight in Romans 12:5, *"So we, being many, are one body in Christ, and everyone members one of another."* (KJV) Can we imagine the power of one? Take the one and divide it up into many parts, and when reassembled together again, it becomes whole and forms one. How fascinating, even in the division, it is still one because its basis equals the sum. This fact may be surprising. GOD has always been awesome, providing the best interest in His creation and our happiness as we are to unify with him and one another. Solidarity with GOD is the key to every situation. As the subject is defined and unveiled, many unanswered questions will open our understanding with GOD's help and hopefully kill some dysfunctional traditions that lead to ungodly and nonbiblical divorces.

Historically, there were some exciting facts uncovered in my literary review. I present these facts as they are written to help understand the impact of how it has played out through the years—starting with some Egyptian history as early as 542 BC, dating back to the 26th Dynasty (7th-6th c. BC). There were writings about ten Demotic divorce writs dating the Persian and Hellenistic periods. These deeds guaranteed the divorced women the right to remarry. The divorce document of an Egyptian named Amenhotep/Amenhotep, dated to 282 BC, reads:

I have abandoned thee (Taapi); I am removed from thee regarding the "law of wife." It is I who has said unto thee: "Make for thyself a husband." I shall not be able to stand before thee in any place where thou goest in order to make for thyself a husband there. I have no claim on earth against thee in the name of "wife" from today onward, instantly, without delay, without a blow. (Reich, 138-39)

As you can see, the husband has released the wife and not allowed her to be in bondage to remain single if she desired to remarry again. It is not stated why he did this. Another tidbit of history continues with Gaius, a jurist of the second century AD, who defined divorce as follows: "The term divortium is derived either from the difference of minds (of the parties) or from the fact that the parties who are tearing the marriage are going their different ways" (Dig. 24.2.2.pr; cited in Rabello, 79). Divorce, like marriage, was a private affair that required no state or religious ratification. It possibly explains why the scripture denotes Joseph was going to put Mary away privily.

Furthermore, in early history of Rome divorce was rare. Despite the assertion of Aulus Gellius that there was not a single case of divorce until 230 BC when Spurius

Carvillius divorced his wife because she was barren, it proceeded into early as the seventh century BC. The Twelve Tables of Law inscribed in 451 BC *record the formula for divorce: "Res tuas tibi habeto," "Take your things to yourself."*

In 307 BC, a senator who put away his wife without a judgment of a tribunal was penalized. In 268 BC, a consul named Publius Sempronius Sophus divorced his wife because she had dared to attend the games without his knowledge. In 1666 BC, Gaius Sulpicius Gallus's consul repudiated his wife because he had detected her in public with her head uncovered.

Society frowned upon the divorce of a virtuous woman who had provided her husband with children. Aemilius Paulus divorced his wife, Papira, who was the mother of very fine children, including the famous Scipio. When his friends derated him for this, he held out a good-looking shoe as an object lesson. He said, "Is it not new? But no one of you can tell me where it pinches my foot?" Plutarch goes on to explain this comment as follows:

"For, as a matter of fact, it is great and notorious faults that separate many wives from their husbands; but the slight and frequent fictions arising from some unpleasantness or incongruity of characters, unnoticed as they may be by everybody else, also produce incurable alienations in those who lives are linked together." (Plu.

Aem. 5.2)

Actual divorces can be documented in literary sources from 100 to 38 BC, number thirty-two, and most of these were made for political reasons. A study of the senatorial aristocracy for the Augustan period to around AD 200 found only 27 attested divorces of 562 women, most from the Julio-Claudian period (31 BC-AD 68). However, this evidence comes only from historical accounts, not inscriptions, as tombstones did not record divorces. In 18 BC, by the lex Iulia de aulteriis, Augustus made adulterium a public crime and required a husband to divorce his wife who had committed adultery. According to this law, if a husband did not divorce an adulterous wife, he would be guilty of lenocinium, "pimping." The adulterous woman would lose half of her dos (dowry) and be exiled to an island, and she could not contract a valid marriage.

A wife could not prosecute her husband for adultery but could divorce him, get her dowry back, and remarry. Under Augustan law, she would have to remarry if she wanted to be eligible to receive legacies. Augustus's Julian law permitted a woman to wait six months after a divorce before remarriage, and his later Pipian Law extended the period to a year and six months. A man who divorced his wife who had committed adultery was obliged to remarry if he did not wish to diminish his ability to receive legacies.

As you can see, this history was twisted, one-sided, and nowhere does it read anything about seeking GOD in the process. Nor does it correctly validate the grounds for divorcement.

Now let us turn our attention to the narrative support of attorney Michael Kuldiner, who wrote an article on November 17, 2012, *History of Divorce, Origins, and Meaning.* This publication gives a brief historical background concerning secular definition of divorce. Here is what he had to say:

"To understand the full history of divorce, first, the term needs to be defined. "Divorce" comes from the Latin word "divortium," which means separation. It is also equivalent to the word "divort" or "divortere." "Di" means a part, and "vertere" means to turn to different ways. "Divertere" is also referred to as the meaning of diverting, turning aside, separating, or leaving one's husband. The word was traced in French vocabulary in the latter part of the 14th century and in the Middle English in the year 1350-1400.

Today, although divorce is expressed or defined in different ways, it expresses a single idea. Most common definitions of divorce include: (1) a judicial declaration dissolving the marriage in whole or in part releasing the husband and wife from the matrimonial obligation to live together; (2) any formal separation of husband and wife according to established customs; and total separation or disunion or to disunite a marital union."

Carefully as we review Mr. Kuldiner's disclosure, it displays both a dictionary and biblical contextual explanation of divorce. Interestingly, both Mr. Kuldiner's and the dictionary terms complement each description of its purpose and mirror his three expressions stated above.

First, let us draw our attention in his first paragraph to the term "vertere," which means "to turn to different ways." If we closely examine his phrase, "to turn to different ways," this is precisely what the enemy magnifies when couples divorce. Both parties should understand that they are turning from the spouse and GOD if they divorce outside of what GOD allows. How so? Matthew 19:6 KJV, "*Wherefore they are no more twain, but one flesh. What therefore GOD hath joined together, let no man put asunder.*" Separation is not an option in this text but the power of one, "NOT TWAIN, BUT ONE FLESH." Therefore, if the two are in agreement to make the union before GOD and believe that he was the cause of their marriage, then by the confession of their words, conforms an oath or vow, making the latter part of the text "LET NO MAN" put asunder to be sustained. Ecclesiastes 5: 1-6 explains the content of empty and vain words or even just speaking in general related to promises or vows that are made and not fulfilled. As our

Creator made us in His image, humanity must understand the purpose of truth and honesty in every aspect of a one-on-one relationship.

From this, humanity consciously and subconsciously thrives on communing with one another. GOD never intended for man to be alone. Even from the Garden of Eden, his actions reflected the continual message that the Ten Commandments affirm. Blinded by their morals, Israel missed the concealed memo and essential factors of "RELATIONSHIPS" that GOD had purposed for them. Simple terms, GOD, man, and others; how they are to relate to each other.

Believers can become deceived just as the Israelites were deceived. We will also miss the message if we're distracted by our morals and worldly traditions. Note, two of the Ten Commandments which relates to oaths: the third commandment which forbids vain promise as He decrees this in Exodus 20:7, "*You shall not take a false oath in the name of the LORD your GOD; for the LORD will not declare him innocent who takes an oath in his name falsely.*" (NIV) How does this relate to marriage and divorce? To answer that question with a clear understanding, we must visit the "Wedding Ceremony and Vows" or oath that is promised at the altar to tie this to Mr. Kuldiner's term "to turn to different ways." As you read through the passages below, notice what starts on good times, later shifting to derogatory terms when the enemy embraced by human emotions turns or tears this momentous celebration to a war zone. Pay close attention to how each word eloquently builds on each promise within the vow/oath.

THE WEDDING CEREMONY

We are gathered here in the presence of GOD, family, and friends to unite _This Man_ and _This Woman__ in holy matrimony. Therefore, marriage is an honorable estate and is not to be entered into lightly, but reverently, advisedly, soberly, and with GOD's blessing. Today, they will receive GOD's greatest gift; another person to share with, grow with, change with, be joyful, and stand with as "ONE" when trials and tribulations enter their lives. Therefore, it is fitting that we should, on this occasion, begin by asking for GOD's blessing on this marriage. Let us pray.

Heavenly Father, we gather to celebrate your gift of love and its presence among us. We rejoice that these two people have chosen to commit themselves to a life of loving faithfulness to one another. We praise you, Lord, for the ways you have touched our lives with loving relationships such as _this man_ and _this woman_, and we give thanks for the special love and friendship you have put in their hearts. Renew within them an affectionate and loving spirit.

Enrich their lives with the gracious gift of your love so that they may embrace others with that same love. May our participation in this celebration of love and commitment give us new joy and responsiveness to their unique relationship in the bond of your grace according to your word. In your loving arms, we pray, Amen.

Marriage is a joyous occasion. It is connected in our thoughts with the charm of love, the warmth of home, and with all that is pleasant, as being one of the most important events of our lives. Its sacredness and unity are the most significant and binding covenant known in human relations.

__This man__ and __This Woman__ , let it be charge to both of you, to remember that your future happiness is to be in mutual consideration, patience, kindness, confidence, and affection. It is the duty of each of you to find your greatest joy in the company of one other, to remember that your love pledged today must remain "undivided" for a lifetime.

Husband, it is your duty, to follow God's plan, to be to a Godly man. Considerate, tender, faithful, and loving husband: to support, guide and cherish your wife in prosperity and trouble; to thoughtfully and carefully enlarge the place she holds in your life; to constantly show her the tokens of your affection, to shelter her from danger, and to love her with an unchangeable love.

Wife, it is your duty, to your husband, to be a Godly woman, Considerate, tender, faithful, and loving wife; to comfort, guide and cherish him in prosperity and trouble; to give your husband the unfailing pieces of evidence of your affection; and to continue making the place he holds in your heart, broader and more profound; to support him, value him and work with him to make your marriage the very best that it can be.

I call your attention to the seriousness of the decision which you both have made and the covenant you both are about to declare before GOD. The vows you are about to take care not to be taken without careful thought, for in them, you are committing yourselves exclusively to one another for as long as you both shall live.

Groom, repeat after me.

I _____, take you, _____, to be my lawfully wedded wife, to have and to hold from this day forward, for better, for worse, for richer, for poorer, in sickness and in health, to love and to cherish, for as long as we both shall live. This is my solemn vow.

Bride, please repeat after me.

I _____, take you, _____, to be my husband, to have and to hold, from this day forward, for better, for worse, for richer, for poorer, in sickness and in health, to love and to cherish, for as long as we both shall live. This is my solemn vow.

You will now exchange rings to symbolize the lifelong commitment and abiding love you as husband and wife have promised to each other.

Groom, please place the ring on _____'s finger and repeat after me.

I give you this ring as a sign of my love and faithfulness.

And Bride, please place the ring on _____'s finger and repeat after me.

I give you this ring as a sign of my love and faithfulness.

Eternal GOD, help _____ and _____ to fulfill the promises they have made here today and reflect your steadfast love in their commitment to each other. Give them kindness and patience, affection and understanding, happiness, and contentment. May their family and friends continue to support them in difficult days so that their love for each other may continue to grow as long as they both shall live. Let us all pray.

Our Father, who art in heaven, Hallowed be thy name, Thy kingdom come, Thy will be done, On Earth, as it is in heaven. Give us this day our daily bread, and forgive us our trespasses,

As we forgive those, who trespass against us, and lead us not into temptation but deliver us from evil.

For thine is the kingdom, And the power, and the glory, Forever and ever. Amen.

DECLARATION OF MARRIAGE

_____ and _____, having witnessed your vows for marriage before GOD and all who are assembled here, by the authority invested in me, I now pronounce you husband and wife. You may now kiss the bride!

It is my pleasure to introduce you to you for the first time… Mr. and Mrs. _____.

Again, these are not mere words but a commitment before witnesses and GOD with his heavenly host. Yes, Satan would like to rift the harmony of twain being one. He knows that unity is all about GOD and his relationship with humanity, and if he can keep this from happening, they will go in different ways.

How so? If the words are pronounced in the ceremony perfidiously, the man and woman speak lies. GOD is about truth, making this conceptional to Satan as he is the Father of all lies. Believers are to cleave and not leave, and if we are a follower of GOD, we cannot go a different way that would lead to the path of divorce. Lies will take us there, and the truth will bring us together as GOD intended. It is a faithful saying that something that is practiced for more than ten days becomes a habit. If the couple recited the ceremony vocabulary frequently, it would leave no room for destruction as their words become more of their lives.

Leading us to the second reference in the ninth commandment, which forbids false oaths, for example, Exodus 20:16, *"You shall not testify falsely [that is, lie, withhold, or manipulate the truth] against your neighbor* (any person)." (AMP) This commandment brings self-evaluation and accountability. The contents of this text will allow an individual to balance their actions as they are communicating with others. Remember, fraudulent activities and lies separate and enable a cavity that dismantles love, trust, peace, and happiness. Not to mention, other spirits take up residence in confusion and perhaps rebellion leading to hearts hardening.

Rules of engagement should always be in every relationship, especially in marriage; this should be established before the "I Do's" occur. If this happens, it is an excellent possibility that the divorce rate would not transpire as often as it does. Mr. Kuldiner's second paragraph shares a revelatory resolution by his perspective on the dictionary definition, utilizing a noun tense of divorce. It states, "a legal dissolution of a marriage by a court or other competent body and separation between things that were or ought to be connected." Notice the noun tense. Its position and meaning are "person, place or thing," and how they contrast to each other.

1. Person [husband and wife] plays equal responsibility in the separation; it is never just one side. Keep in mind that the twain shall be one, and therefore each has to take part in the actions involved to keep the unity. Here is where the rules of engagement need to transpire, and if done correctly, it will conquer and defeat the disconnection. There is nothing as crucial as putting faith and work in action. Indeed, the road can become rough, and couples may find it hard to survive, but GOD's word is superior to divorce, and the ultimate goal is to avoid the very essence of divorce.

2. Place [society...aka, judicial decoration and established customs], GOD should be the center and leader of marriage when it comes to a husband and wife. Any perceptions of society's traditions or new norms, outsider's opinion [especially if they are not married themselves] should be expelled and never infiltrate the sanctity of marriage. Humanism is a form of cancer naturally and spiritually when it

is in operation where GOD should be essential. Believers are never to take a back seat and compromise to what is comfortable for our societal norms. Stinking thinking gets humanity into trouble, and GOD certainly is not pleased being pushed aside as he is jealous. We should have nothing before him, definitely not the ideals of humanity.

3. Thing [unlawful activities, total separation or disunion or to disunite a marital union].

The thing is an ugly monster waiting to unleash and tucked from its hidden sources, springs the root of unlawful activities as time progresses in a marriage. When this happens, early prevention against divorce must and should be explored. The starting place is always the two individuals looking within and not blaming the other. Have a soul-searching expedition asking GOD to reveal all that is not pleasing or not like him. If we are to lay aside every weight and sin that so easily besets us, exploiting harmful spirits that somehow attached themselves to our lives would be appreciated as GOD discloses for castration of the enemy.

Divorce can be deadly. The verb tense [showing action] of the word as separate or dissociate (something) from something else, which collaborates with the term's Latin origin, focusing on the prefix of the word "di" or "div," whose root translated refers to the meaning: separated or divide. This prefix "div," when viewed by other terms, unfolds some mysteries that lead to an open portal of rifting a harmonious institute of marriage to be nullified, divided, segregated, keep apart, isolated, disconnected, severed, dismantled, scattered, detached, disembodied, disengaged, decoupled, disjointed, split, broken up, disassociated, unyoked and unlinked.

All nineteen characteristics are associated with the devil's attack to abolish unity, beginning with Eden's garden's first marriage, staining humanity even until today. Woven in the stain of sin came shame, disloyalty, dishonesty, lies, deceitfulness, persecution, dysfunction, and many other nasty elements that could be listed. Psychologically, no one wants to admit that they have these traits within them or their relationship, many deny such factors. Satan stands by and watches as these issues are avoided and grows with the intent to steal, kill, and destroy. Believers need to be ever so discerning and educated to the facts that leads to divorce. For example, in the National Institutes of Health (NIH) June 2013 publication, one of society's professional organizations performed a survey and deliberated their real reasons for divorce. According to their research studies, these are the findings:

"Major contributors for divorce" are as follows: lack of commitment (75.0%), infidelity/extra-marital affairs (59.6%), too much arguing or conflict (57.7%), marrying too young (45.1%), economic hardship (36.7%), substance abuse (34.6%), domestic violence (23.5%), lack of support from family members, little or no premarital education and religious differences. The article stated that the last three categories were endorsed less than 20% of the time. No matter how our society presents its cause, it is indisputable that the devil is behind every excuse and structural tendencies to promote divorce. Yet manifestation of "div" and its attributes continues to discombobulate marriages every day.

So, who is to blame? Indeed, it is not the man or the woman but the devil, again, as stated earlier, who came to steal, kill, and destroy. Simple, if he can cause one-third of heavenly angels to be kicked out with him, eternally separated from the presence of GOD, what makes us think he was just satisfied with one-third when he wanted all. We must realize that the more he can keep humanity divided in any form, closed-minded, the powerless in unity, the more he uses these tools to keep divorce to continue to rise. This demonic spirit will continue to hinder love, harmony, and loyalty from flowing one to another. So, when a couple realizes this root of division has sprung up in their marriage, they must work together to drive out every seed of wickedness to defeat this ugly, evil monster called divorce.

Can this be stopped? It most certainly can. But it will

take GOD, the discipline of men and women submitting to one another and following the prescriptions of GOD'S WAY; and leaving out legalism. It may seem hard but with determination, ALL THINGS ARE POSSIBLE!!

"Your LIFE will NOT break or pop because of the problems that are in YOUR life. God will NEVER leave you, nor FORSAKE you."

– Pastor Nikia Smith

CHAPTER TWO

Traditional Misconceptions

T raditions, traditions, traditions, some good and some not so good, but when it comes to our salvation, we need to take a stand, ridding ourselves from misconceptions and errors of the norm. For too long, humanity has established its system of what they feel will be the correct answers to world problems; however, this concept is as dangerous as a live stick of dynamite. Cancerous to the lives that are touched by ignorance, selfishness, and other unassuming behaviors, continues to carry over into relationships and marriages as they end in ruins. Such traditional teaching has paralyzed personalities, corrupting hearts, minds, souls, and spiritual maturity in GOD. Our creator has much to say about this, and he certainly does not want us to perish because we lack knowledge on overcoming such matters.

Proverbs 4:23 instructs us in this manner, *"Guard your heart above all else, for it determines the course of your life."* (NLT): the first word says it all – "Guard," to keep safe from harm or danger; protect; watch over, prevent something from happening, and take precautions to disallow outside intruders. If it were not so, it would not have been stated in the word to perform it. Put it this way; this is not a statement but a commandment. Believers should not hesitate to exercise the power that he has given us. That power is the "HOLY GHOST," and we can do anything if we profess that the greater one is within us. GOD has a great cloud of witnesses throughout this world. Many have remained silent and perhaps afraid to share their testimony about how they have overcome. Whatever the reason, help has arrived. My assignment is to release the wisdom that I have gained from my journey to help combat and eradicate the traditional misconceptions concerning marriage and divorce through GOD's anointed Word.

Why be afraid to break cycles that have been misguided by unhealthy and unchallenged practices? Does a person have to accept that it is the way it is and let the poison destroy them? The aftermath of damage control stemmed before Noah's flood and countless other passages in the bible. Fear of but, fear of what if, fear of people, fear of self, and the most damnable believing the devil's lies that you can't be free or victorious. One passage of scripture that I like in particular is when Jesus put the Pharisees and scribes to shame when they asked Him, *"Why walk not thy disciples according to the tradition of the elders, but eat bread with unwashen hands?"* (Mark 7:5 KJV) Indeed, there was some unhealthy and misguided thinking.

Why was it necessary to approach Jesus and point out the disciples' errors and conduct?

Was it so much that their hands were dirty they couldn't get over, or were they trying to downplay the disciple's character? Jesus knew who He was dealing with and how to handle the foolishness projecting from these religious men. Had they discerned in the correct spirit that they picked the wrong season to come to Jesus with their carnal judgment, I believe they would have done things differently.

Were they just upset that those rules were broken or was the matter more about them as much as they made it appear about GOD's laws? Yet, they were not one hundred percent obeying the rules themselves but had the nerve to point the finger at the flaws of others. Careful, this runaway spirit pops up too frequently in marriages, and we need to use this passage as a mirror to trample out traditions in our own lives.

Did they ever give it a thought or consider what

motivated them in their actions? Isaiah 5:21 was the perfect answer for them, *"Woe unto them that are wise in their own eyes, and prudent in their sight!* "(KJV) and *"Those who think they are wise are as good as dead, those who think they possess understanding."* (NET) Humanity is guilty of this same action and our self-will allows pride to dictate our efforts in this same manner.

How cunning will the devil lead an individual to make a fool out of themselves? This question was presented in a public setting, and others were about to see them be put to an open shame. Judging by their actions, I believe that they were concerned about the legalism of rules. The issue of the disciples' unwashed hands was just a distraction to keep attention off their faults and make them appear right before the people. I also come to this conclusion because, as you read further in that same chapter, Jesus rebukes them and calls them "hypocrites" and confronts them about holding on to the traditions of men and laying aside the commandments of GOD. He let them know they were so vain and carnal-minded that they could not see their faults but could point out others' errors. Today, this same type of deception still plagues our society because of those who carry on unbeneficial philosophies.

Since our subject is about divorce, we must deal with it head-on concerning the misconceptions about who can and cannot exercise the right to do so. Lives marred by authorities having placed themselves in GOD's place and not considering their livelihood have been seduced by their ideology. Again, men and women need to take a stand, break cycles, and take back their lives to regain their freedom of strongholds.

Colossians 2:8 KJV warns us first of all about this very thing: *"Beware lest any man spoil you through philosophy and vain deceit, after the tradition of men, after the rudiments of the world, and not after Christ."* Weymouth New Testament translates this same warning as such: *"Take care lest there be someone who leads you away as prisoners by means of his philosophy and idle fancies, following human traditions and the world's crude notions instead of following Christ."* These warnings certainly are clear that we cannot allow traditional misconceptions to cloud our views with society or tainted religious beliefs regarding divorce's philosophy. Think about it.

Who, in their right mind, wants to be a prisoner or be enslaved by someone? No one wants to be enslaved. However, people are driven by what others think if they do something different or outside of what societal norms say we must do. This in and of itself is slavery and most certainly a stronghold.

I am 150% convinced that because I allowed myself to go through the process of pain, battling my emotions, and the purging of GOD, through the transformation of my flaws, I am being used as a vessel for His glory. Trust me, it was not a pleasant or comfortable ride, but I made it. By now, I am sure you are asking yourself, what was the secret behind breaking traditions and misconceptions? Remember, in the previous chapter, I stated some might not agree, but please keep an open mind to my words and GOD's spirit as you read on. Beginning with 1 Corinthians 7:16, the chiseling and breaking of the fallow grounds freeing me from traditional habits. I will continue with more in-depth insight into the next chapter but for now, let me give you this piece of the testimony.

The question within this particular text was explosive. To understand how it gripped my heart, I will use several translations to express the understanding that I received. I never experienced such insight as GOD awakened me as the anointing fell, speaking expressively about my thoughts on wanting to divorce my husband. Scripture after scripture continues to come, and as I share this prophetic understanding, positively, this speaks to us Women of GOD (men there is a part for you as well). Pay close attention to what the spirit of GOD is saying to us women: 1 Corinthians 7:16: *"For what knowest thou, O wife, whether thou shall save thy husband?"* (KJV) or *"Don't you wives realize that your husbands might be saved because of you?"* (NLT) or how about this translation, *"For what assurance have you, O woman, as to whether you will save your husband?"* (WNT) and *"You never know, wife: The way you handle this might bring your husband not only back to you but to GOD."* (MSG)

For six months to three years, this scripture ministered to me as a lingering question, "How would you know?" My answer would always be, I would not know if I gave up. But I kept trying to look for a way out because that seems to be more comfortable than going through the process of doing it GOD's way. Surprisingly, I had no clue that GOD was giving me a recipe, and I had only one ingredient to break a cycle that had plagued my family from my grandparents, my parents, and now I was facing the same issue. The more I prayed, the more I wrestled with GOD concerning why He would not allow me to divorce my husband. My anger grew, and I felt victimized because I wanted out. GOD was answering me, but I could not hear Him speaking because I allowed society's traditions to be my scapegoat and the justification of my flesh dictating the desired outcome. GOD wanted accountability for my actions. I was behaving just like the Pharisees. I sought a reason to point out all the errors of my husband and not look at what part I had played in this rift in my marriage. Preaching and on my way to HELL!

My hypocritical thinking caused unnecessary heartache and pain to my children, my marriage, and myself. I thought because he was not a believer and living up to my standards, I had a right to take matters into my own hands. I was walking on dangerous ground allowing the enemy to steal my anointing, soul, and the entire family. Remember, the devil comes to steal, kill, and destroy, but I was helping him. Just as Eve assisted the devil in the Garden of Eden, she presented the fruit to her husband - which later separated us from GOD. Women, we have more power than we think, and the enemy knows this. Read and reread the passage until it ignites a fire that burns all the enemies' persuasion out! This deceitful and cunning spirit was instrumental in the great fall; however, it does not have to be ours. Use all ingredients prescribed in GOD's word, and we will have the VICTORY.

Men, you have not escaped from your roles and responsibilities as what is essential in this matter. Remember, God made you first, and you have the ultimate responsibility to protect what God handed over to you in the garden, authority over the earth. This means whatever grounds you have possessed as part of your grounds to keep, take a stand and don't do as Adam did and allow the devil to come in and just wreak havoc in your life, wife, or marriage.

"Be strong in the Lord, and in the power of his might..." (Ephesians 6:10 KJV) is what God wanted from the beginning and allowed that sanctity of oneness to abide with him, you, and your mate. If you lose sight of fellowship and relationship with God speaking to you,

this opens the door for anything to happen.

Yes, your mate may be doing things that you do not like but the blame game got Adam and Eve nowhere. For this cause, everyone should learn a lesson that we MUST be responsible for our actions, and we have a choice in the matter to not allow anyone or anything to separate us from our responsibility and to the obedience to GOD. Let them have the write-up, and judgment comes to a reaction for the wrong actions. So why be part of that? We as a people love praise and rewards. Divorce does not give either one of these things, only sorrow and death. Just as it did when sin entered the garden, that put a division between GOD's divine relationship with his creation; however, it did not kill his love for them. So, in essence, if a couple that is having trouble will go back and examine the underlying conditions from the garden, then look at themselves, half of the battle is conquered. With GOD, ALL THINGS ARE POSSIBLE if you allow it to manifest as He directs you. There is more to this recipe as we continue.

"When you hurt, God feels the PAIN. You're His most prized POSSESSION. You're His CHILD."

– Spiritual Inspiration

CHAPTER THREE

Is it Fornication or Adultery?

We have explored some historical background in the previous chapters, unraveled some misconceptions and traditions, and defined divorce. We will go deeper into the topic to better understand what is not taught in society or even hardly in Christendom.

Once again, I would like to make this appeal to you, the reader. You may disagree with the content of these pages; however, be open and allow the Spirit of GOD to speak to you as you read. I am sure you will be amazed. Here we go. We will start with Matthew 19:9 of the King James Version (KJV) and then review the Amplified Bible version (AMP): "*And I say unto you, Whosoever shall put away his wife, except it be for fornication, and shall marry another, committeth adultery: and whoso marrieth her which is put away doth commit adultery."* (KJV) or *"I say to you, whoever divorces his wife, except for sexual immorality, and marries another woman commits adultery."* (AMP)

What does this passage mean? Religiously this scripture has been taught that you can divorce because of adultery. WRONG! That is not what this passage says, and this is why it is important to study and do background research on words and the content of their meaning. So, to correctly divide and interpret this scripture of its contextual meaning, it must be broken down. What does it say? It says that they can divorce, and that is, on the grounds of "Fornication," not "Adultery," this can be tricky, and here is where the enemy gets believers off track. He twists the words in our minds to read what we want to hear, just as he did Mother Eve in the garden. Our emotions perceive what we desire, and it does not allow our spirit to divide and discern through the Holy Ghost. Therefore, when we take a closer look at the text, it tells us that: when a person remarries after they have divorced, not for the reason of fornication, they are the Adulterer.

SHOCKING, I will say again, the person who divorces not for the grounds of fornication and remarries again is the person committing adultery, or the person who marries the put-away wife is the adulterer! It cannot get any plainer than it's written. We don't see the truth because that is not what we want when we are hurting, angry, bitter, resentful, or the like. That is why the enemy tries to keep us in the dark concerning the Word of God and wants us to wear it loosely and not bind it in our hearts.

After I read this over and over, it still did not make sense to me, so I asked GOD, "How do married people commit fornication if they are married? Would that not be adultery?" Here is where the Holy Spirit began to download in me through the word and spoke to me directly. The spirit of GOD started teaching me what fornication is, and this is what I learned through my time in prayer and researching as he led me on this journey.

Fornication in Greek means "porneia," the original meaning of the is "to prostitute" or "to sell." It can also mean pornography, pedophilia, promiscuity, homosexuality, lesbianism, incest, premarital sex, bestiality, or possibly idolatry. All depict erotic behavior intended to cause sexual excitement or acts sensually to arouse a quick, intense emotional reaction. Vines Expository Dictionary defines it as "illicit sexual intercourse." In Merriam-Webster Dictionary, fornication is consensual sexual intercourse between two people who are not married to each other. These listings only give some ideas on the meaning, but there is more. Generally, the traditional teaching down through the years has only taught fornication as it was defined by

Merriam-Webster's version of sexual relations of those single and nothing else. I have never heard it taught in the manner I am about to explain, and that was only once, in a seminar months after God had opened my understanding to it. I thought I was hallucinating and even told God that if I start teaching this or even mentioning such things, people will think I am a false teacher, that I made this up by myself, or have lost my mind. That did not stop God from continuing to pour into me month after month until I received all that he had and am still learning today. The Bible certainly answers what fornication means and how it relates to Matthew 19:9 concerning divorce. We will cover six topics of fornication as it pertains to marriage and define how a married person can commit the act of fornication which are biblical grounds that will allow divorce to be legal in perspective according to the Word of God.

IDOLATRY

The following scriptures outline instructions on how GOD does not want humanity to worship false gods: [Deuteronomy 14:1-2, Leviticus 19:4, 28, and 20:5-6] However, we will visit this text for now to start our journey of understanding. *Thou shalt have no other gods before me. Thou shalt not make unto thee any graven image, or any likeness of any thing that is in the heaven above, or that is in the earth beneath, or that is in the water under the earth: "Thou shalt not bow down thyself to them, nor serve them: for I am the LORD thy GOD am a jealous GOD, visiting the iniquity of the fathers upon the children unto the third and fourth generation of them that hate me..."* (Exodus 20: 3-5 KJV) The purpose of the Ten Commandments or the Ten Laws of God, should always be part of a believer's life. It not only ties into our relationship with God, but it has a significant role in all types of relationships. How uniquely does GOD himself give Moses these commandments and laws so that humanity would know how to carry out a proper relationship across the board.   GOD is all about commitment, one on one and nothing else. Therefore, idolatry in its connection to fornication, humanity has diluted what God wants and has allowed their perception to become geared in the direction of extreme admiration, love, or reverence for something or someone outside of their relationship to GOD or even their mate whom they have vowed to be committed too.

These attributes transform into pagan worship and traditions not associated with holy living or obedience to GOD. Consider this when it comes to idolatry in terms of fornication in a marriage. When a husband or a wife's behavior becomes estranged, they no longer want to give reverence to GOD first, then their spouse. How so? The spouse who finds themselves not wanting to continue practicing holy living or making excuses not to engage even in Christian activities opens a demonic portal to allow the enemy to come in with subtle little spirits that we will discuss a little later. Many of the warning signs are always present but often ignored. Little tiny things, such as prayer time or bible reading, begins to diminish, not to mention fasting or worship service. Remember, the Bible tells us that the small foxes destroy the vines, and this vine happens to be a marriage the enemy is after and uses this subtle tool of idolatry to get a firm hold on the weaker mate. Sadly, the history of the church teaching never took the time to define idolatry and connect it to the act of fornication. Can you imagine how many marriages could have been saved or how many believers could have received the necessary deliverance knowing such information?

The time has come for this little secret of truth to give the clarion call to believers who find themselves unable to control a simple matter, to seek help, and seek it fast. When seemingly isolated, little innocent things stem up, don't just tuck it away and let it lay dormant, confront it. Idolatry is dangerous, so be cautious. When you recognize them be willing to break the cycles of falsehoods that have bound many for decades.

Leaders take a stand! When a couple seeks to divorce, take time to survey and find out the root cause, such as this spirit and the others we will cover. Why is this so important? Brother James says this in chapter one, verse fourteen: *"But every man is tempted, when he is drawn away of his own lust, and enticed.*" (KJV) "Notice, he speaks of three warnings: being tempted, drawn away, and enticed. I would like to call it "Delilah," the spirit that keeps nagging until it is in control as it weakens the individual's mind to lure in its traps.

Spirits such as those who encourage people to live their lives dependent upon their horoscope, witchcraft, tattooing, fads, or seeking a medium are part of self-gratification. The desire to continue indulging or participating in its acts causes an arousing or excitement to fulfill the appetite or temptation as it has entered through these evil spiritual portals. These spirits themselves become controlling and compromise the morals of the individual. Such have crept into the "four walls of the Church" and casually taken a seat where GOD should be. The believer no longer finds anything wrong with their actions and is ignorant of the history of each type of spirit naturally or spiritually. Also, they find themselves making excuses not to believe that God is not real or they can be helped with anything that they are struggling with. THIS IS A SURE SIGN AND PROBLEM, again get help and get it fast!

This self-gratifying spirit seeks attention, and the more it intensifies, the more it becomes the central focus of their needs as the "I" spirit begins to drive. Pride and all its cousins move in, and an explosion has happened in the marriage before you know it. Hidden and blinded to the truth, the warnings are there, screaming louder and louder. If you see these signs, seek help because souls are at state. If not careful when they are intimate, these spirits can transfer and cause spiritual sickness. The nature of idolatry can be conquered, and there is no reason that any couple should allow this type of spirit to survive in their marriage. Make sure that the wise council you are seeking are well versed in the word on casting out spirits and know how to minister in the delivering process.

INCEST

In Deuteronomy 27: 20, 22, and 23, Leviticus 18: 6-16, 19:29, 20: 11, 12, 17, 19 and 20, Ezekiel 22: 10-11 all have examples of sexual perversion and lawlessness of Israel's disobedience to GOD. Because of such actions, this spirit has imprisoned so many people leaving them wounded for life and sometimes have never been healed or delivered.

Incest is defined as sexual relations between classed people being too closely related to marry each other; the crime of having sexual intercourse with parents, child, siblings, grandchildren, and other close relatives. From this monstrous spirit can birth other demons, as listed in the passage. Its dark root of evil venom steals life and happiness and even death in some cases, accompanying its actions. This does not seem to be common; but it does and has happened. There are so many who are suffering because someone in their family violated them, their world is shatter and turned upside down and silence seems to be the norm of protection when it is really a killer.

Many little boys and little girls are disabled due to this fierce spirit. They have concealed their terrible, deep dark secret, and as they grow into teens and adulthood, their future relationships suffer from mistrust, hurt, anger, and other undesirable behaviors. Some may find themselves acting promiscuous, sometimes accepted, and never considered as a cry for help. As incest relates to marriages and divorces, the hidden turmoil raging inside its victim is like a volcano ready to erupt over a situation they had no control over and wanting help but not knowing how to get it, and some are no longer the victim but have become the perpetrator. The guilt and shame follow like a shadow, sometimes seen and sometimes not. Believers, please understand how this immoral act ties into fornication and should be acknowledged if and when it arises in the marriage and leads to divorce. Incest is real, and it has happened and does exist in the "four walls of the Church."

Can you imagine this happening in one of the local churches in your city or town? What an outrage to know that a family is suffering at the hand of such demonic activities. How distressing was this when I came into the knowledge of an individual that I thought was strange because of how the person was a loner and how they carried themselves. Not knowing that both them and their siblings were being abused and molested by their father. Someone had to know about this, and it amazes me that nothing was done. This horrible secret was kept for years, and even the mother of the children was being abused. Many of the family members have suffered mental disorders and other things as a result of incest. I did not find this out until later in my saved life, and when I did, I felt so horrible. But one thing is for sure, I made it my business to apologize to the person for saying and thinking bad things about them.

One never knows what an individual has been facing behind closed doors or even in their past, and believers need to understand the operation of an incest spirit to help a loved one receive the help they need and possibly deliver them from divorce.

RAPE

Rape is not far from incest and often overlaps in some instances – [Judges 19:22-30,20:5, Genesis 19:8, 30-35, 2 Samuel 13:1-15, Isaiah 13:15-16, Lamentations 5:11, and Zechariah 14:2]. This spirit drives the person to force themselves on their victims without consent because of overwhelming sexual emotions. Those that have experienced this horrible treatment are also left feeling abandoned, resentful, and ashamed. This is not something that is so easily expressed when one has been raped or molested. The horrific experience is enough as it torments and haunts individuals for much of their lives. Even so, left unattended, the infection of its bitter roots germinates into an "STD", a spiritual trans-sending demon, and over time becomes the works of the flesh. Now the works of the flesh are manifest, which are these: "*...adultery, fornication, uncleanness, lasciviousness, idolatry, witchcraft, hatred, variance, emulations, wrath, strife, seditions, heresies, envyings, murders, drunkenness, revellings, and such...*" (Galatians 5:19-21 KJV.)

Here is an eye opener: as I continue with this topic, I will describe other characteristics as it relates to rape. Earlier, it was discussed that fornication originally means prostitution or selling. If a child is offered as a sexual favor in exchange or is a token in an agreement, the giving person is committing rape. This also applies if the wife or husband is offered for sex to anyone outside of their marriage, such as spouse swapping. Here is where the offence becomes surface, the offeree may not perform the act; however, it causes the child to be traumatized because the child has no voice in the matter. The legal term for this is guilt by association. Therefore, the offeree's involvement is just as if they are the person doing the deed.

An example of this is child trafficking for underground prostitution or even prostituting in the form of pornography.

Shocking as this may sound, if more men and women in Christendom would be transparent and speak out against such ferocious treatment, that they have experienced, they could not only help others but deliver themselves. Instead, they allow their past or even events in their marriage to cripple them as they walk around like a time bomb waiting to explode and spew their poisonous venom on unexpected innocents. Yes, such behavior has crept into the four walls of the church and has been kept silent and hidden under the proverbial rug for centuries. Biblically, the Bible gives it another name: ravish – to seize or take by violence or force. This is what happened in the case of Tamar; her brother raped her, and this led to other spirits springing forth as a result of such actions. Surprisingly as it is kept, this is what happens when a selfish nature begins to dominate one's mindset. It can manifest in many ways by the works of the flesh, as we stated earlier according to Galatians chapter five.

So, when the discovery of rape, past or present in a relationship is revealed, it is very shameful and a blow to the marriage. This is when the husband and the wife need like never before, cling to their mate to get help that is critically needed and life sustaining. Therefore, it is the upmost important both mates agree and to get the proper counseling and assistance for spiritual and natural healing. The effluence of a rape victim emanates the torment they live daily because of what happened to them and becomes the internal mirror in which they see and acknowledge themselves. They begin to believe what happened to them is their fault! They identify themselves as a nasty person, someone deserving of this atrocity. This outlandish, all-encompassing fornicated spirit reeks with the resentful malice of revenge, hatred, and other associated demonic spirits. Can you think of anyone who wants their marriage to be infiltrated by this nightmare when it should be filled with the enjoyment of intimacy?

When a person has received treatment in the right way, they will undoubtedly see the fulfillment of God's love through oneness to flourish in our lives and relationship with him. Jesus said My Father and I are One. So can we mirror this statement and be one with Him as we surrender all the baggage that destroys couples and enslaves them to traditions and secrets that haunt and taunt their marriages. Be free, not from your mate; instead, divorce the spirit of rape! This demonic spirit is what the enemy wants to use as a wildcard of excuses not to love but destroy marital relationships to keep them from being unified as God intended.

BESTIALITY

This is one encounter that is not taught or talked about concerning sin or fornication. Don't think it is strange that this is on the list of actions as it pertains to fornication. If this were not so, it would not have been mentioned in the Bible in Exodus 22:19, Leviticus 18:22-23, 20:15-16, Deuteronomy 27:21.

Within the above referenced passages, God clearly expresses that sexual intercourse between a human and animals is forbidden. This may sound crazy, but some have been led to this type of behavior and are unsatisfied with their natural affections. Much of this comes from Greek mythology beliefs and practices that happened during Roman rule. During that time, it was common in pagan worship and idolatry. This unveiled erotic emotion causes the individual to have a sexual appetite to engage in defiling sexual acts with animals for self-gratification which leads them away from GOD resulting in fornication.

As stated in Ecclesiastes 1:9 TV, "*What has been, that will be; what has been done, that will be done. - Nothing is new under the sun; the future only repeats the past.*"

Again, this demonic activity may not be discussed that much today; but that does not mean it does not exist. I will even go as far as stating that some diseases transcend from humans sleeping with animals. Secretly, some may be keeping this on the down-low yet struggle with the entanglement to be delivered from this demonic stronghold.

ORGIES

Orgy in its plural content "orgies" meaning: a wild party, especially involving excessive drinking and unrestrained sexual activity. Historically, secret ceremonial rites were held in honor of a deity among the Greeks and Romans, especially those who worship Dionysus, or Bacchus. This is characterized by ecstatic singing, dancing, and often revelry, drunkenness, or carousel as referenced in Romans 13:13 and Galatians 5:21.

Although the Bible does not exactly utilize the word Orgy in the context in which we may think; however, it does allude to it by the usage via the terms reviling or carousing. "*Let us walk properly as in the daytime, not in orgies and drunkenness, not in sexual immorality and sensuality, not in quarreling and jealousy.*" (Romans 13:13 ESV)

Examine the account according to Esther 1:8-9 of King Ahasuerus' behavior after seven days of drunkenness and the suggestion of his friends to do a shameful deed towards Queen Vashti.

So many point fingers at her behavior and skip over the

king's behavior. Still, when you carefully examine the context of the scripture, one will see that it clearly defines that there were orgies taking place. The king wanted her to parade around in front of all his friends with just her crown on, to show off her beauty (nakedness) as if she was his merchandise that he was flaunting and bragging about in the text. How could this be love or protection, when such behavior was degrading to the Queen and her womanhood. It there is a time not to share, it is most certain the rules should be used in intimacy of the marriage. Keep it scared only between husband and wife and NO ONE ELSE.

Galatians 5:21 also states *"…envy, murder, drunkenness, wild partying, and things like that. I am telling you now, as I have told you in the past, that people who practice such things will not inherit the kingdom of God."* (ISV) or *"…envying, murder, drunkenness, carousing, and similar things. I am warning you, as I had warned you before: Those who practice such things will not inherit the kingdom of God!"* (NET)

Those who practice this unclean and selfish spirit most certainly commit fornication, and it is a sure sign of unfaithfulness behavior, leading to the destruction and death of a marriage.

We can see how this text aligns with what was going on in Esther chapter one. I would be displeased if my mate would like to share our intimacy with others and disregard that it is a bond of oneness, of fellowship sacred to GOD.

As this relates to God, it is with utmost confidence that we should have no other gods besides Him. Why? A marital relationship should mirror the type of relationship with our Heavenly Father. We should not flaunt or cheat our mates of oneness as unto God. Not only because he is jealous, but because it is a full circle showing intimacy with him, through the relationship of oneness, unification, and solidarity of commitment. This act in itself; separates and disrespects God in all manner if the two are to be one, when others are involved.

HOMOSEXUALITY

When it comes to the topic, there is no doubt of how God feels about it. Beginning with Genesis 2:18, 21, 24, 25: *"[18]And the LORD GOD said, it is not good that man should be alone; I will make him an help meet for him. [21]And the LORD GOD caused a deep sleep to fall upon Adam, and he slept: and he took one of his ribs, and closed up the flesh instead thereof, And the rib, which the LORD God had taken from man, made he a woman, and brought her unto the man. [24]Therefor shall a man leave his father and his mother and shall cleave unto his wife; and they shall be one flesh. [54]And they were both naked, the man and his wife, and were not ashamed."* [Reference scriptures: Leviticus 18:22, 20:13, 1Corinthians 6:9-10,

Romans1:26-27, 1Timothy 1:8-11]

GOD made a male and a female to enjoy one another. We can see this, as he has stated, "THEY (meaning MALE and FEMALE) shall be one flesh - not male/male or female/female. There is a precise distinction between what GOD wanted and what his plans were and still is. Examine Genesis 1:27 the purpose of his design for MALE and FEMALE, I quote, *"So GOD created man in his own image, in the image of God created he him; male and female created he them.* And GOD blessed them, [AGAIN meaning MALE and FEMALE] *Be fruitful and multiply, and replenish the earth, and subdue it; and have dominion over...."* These passages alone destroy the account that men should be with men and women with women. Our society has truly enabled the enemies' diabolic plot to sever the relationship with GOD. They have become weaker in GOD and wiser to the things they want and Satan's deceptive spirit keeps them blinded to God's sole purpose of humanity on the earth. There is no way to misunderstand what GOD has so plainly stated. MALE and FEMALE are precisely what he wanted and designed for marriage to be from the foundation of the world and to be carried throughout a lifetime, to be fruitful and multiply. Male/male and female/female relationships cannot fulfill this commandment. John 14:15, 21 and 15:10 repeatedly emphasizes that if we love God, we will keep His commandments. Thereby, identifying homosexuality as anti-God.

To further support GOD's design for a lasting marriage, 1 Corinthian 7:2 -3 ESV, "*Nevertheless, to avoid fornication, let every man have his own wife, and let every woman have her own husband. Let the husband render unto the wife due benevolence: and likewise, also the wife unto the husband.*" Today, it puzzles me how our society seems to think that GOD was confused and that they can change it because of their motives. Unquestionably, the devil is behind this deep root of wickedness. God has given an example of how an entire city was destroyed due to this wicked, perverse spirit of homosexuality. The Bible says that it is an abomination; it disgusts GOD, and he hated the likes thereof. So why would someone want to be addressed or hated when they can be favored and blessed. Yes, God loves everyone, however, He hates sin. Homosexuality is sin. An act of evil which is fornication. So, no matter how our society has legalized it, made it okay, or even acted like it does not exist, it does not change GOD's word one bit.

"What if DIVORCE is not so much about UNBECOMING everything that isn't really YOU, the person God created you to be and the POINT of all of this is to PUT you on the PATH to which you BELONG."

— Jen Grice

CHAPTER FOUR

God's Perception and Ground Rules

Now that we have discovered the history, meaning, and attributes of divorce, what now?

Can your life or others be the same now that you have a different perspective than what had been handed down from generation to generation and from centuries and beyond? When it comes to the truth of GOD's word being taught correctly, it should always bring about change in the believer's life. When a believer states that they have given their life over to GOD, they say that they have the indwelling presence of the Holy Spirit, who leads and guides them into all truth. However, it is up to the believer to show some sign of His presence in and over their life. The spirit of GOD helps the believer to decipher or decern what is right and wrong. GOD will not leave any believer in the dark about anything from complexity to simplicity regarding his Word. This would be our portion, if we would only walk in His spirit and LET THE WORD WORK IN US AS WE LIVE THE WORD. Thereby understanding and internalizing what he said in Philippians 4:13 that we can do all things in Him as He strengthens us.

There is no need to stay in the dark and be troubled by old traditions or emotional, idealistic teaching that damaged many lives. God wants His people to be free, not enslaved to things or ways that He has not set. Far too long, the easy way out has been the solution, and society has made it easy to appease the flesh. Whatever happened to the saying that anything worth having is worth working or fighting for? All we can hear nowadays is that I am tired, and nobody knows what I am going through or why I must be the bigger person. Going back to what was said in earlier chapters, how can born-again believers who confess to being "SAVED" or a "CHRISTIAN," (being Christ-like) have such ungodly spirits dictating what their actions are to be? Do the couple not see each other as a brother or sister in Christ? Do they not realize, as a married couple, they are accountable to one another and are one flesh? Yes, the husband and wife may be two separate individuals in the natural, but in the spirit, they are one as this is how GOD designed marriage to operate.

God never intended for us to be lonely, unlearned, or

even destroyed. In other words, he designed us with emotions to love, be faithful, and obedient unto him. Every sacrifice that we make to gain more insight concerning him and his love, the more he will unveil the truth to how love will help us to conquer separation or unjust divorce. Scriptures such as Genesis 2:24, Matthew 19:5 – 6, Mark 10:8, and 1Corinthians 7:2 have the secret formula to help win the battle of divorce.

What is the mystery embedded within the content of these scriptures? To unveil, I must revisit the visitation of God as he spoke to me during my separation from my husband in 2005. I cannot recall whether I was asleep or awake, but I thoroughly remembered the download to open my understanding. I had an issue with intimacy and the likes thereof. Although I had indulged in sex, my mind would always somehow reflect on the past when I had been raped. That is why I could release such wisdom in this area earlier in chapter three. This became a downfall and a hindrance in my marriage and caused damage to my relationship with my husband. I needed help and kept the secret for year. Recently, about two or three years ago, I told my father of the incident. You could only imagine how he looked or felt when this was revealed to him, coming from his daughter and his first-born child. Nevertheless, this may sound strange and difficult to understand; but divine intervention was most certainly taking place. I had given my life to Christ not knowing God's plan for me. Without realizing it, I had become a sacrificial witness for Him. God allowed me to share my testimony to help someone else to be made whole, and to discover what He could do if they allow Him to undo that same hurt and pain that haunted me and heal.

Here is how the process begins: first, it is vital that every married couple understands Genesis 2:24 KJV, "...*therefore shall a man leave his father and mother and shall cleave unto his wife; and they shall be one flesh.*" We read this scripture so casually and think that if we understand "One Flesh," well, it is more than what meets the eyes. This is a hidden treasure, and we need some keys to unlock what is within the confounds of this text. I will briefly explain those keys, but for now, we will speak on Leviticus 17:11 that will help us understand "One Flesh."

This passage explains that the life of the flesh is in the blood. Most individuals don't think about this because I certainly did not give it a thought until God enlighten me that the one-flesh was a form of worship that we call sex or making love.

This form of worship was designed so that God commanded Adam and Eve according to Genesis 1:27 – 28, to replenish the Earth. Man and Woman were made for worship, and at that time, sin had not transpired. So, as He gave them the commandment, this was to show honor to God, in the beauty of purity as they were made in the likeness of Him. Remember, God is about commitment and oneness, so there had to be some bonding going on. Also, remember that God met with Adam in the cool of the day for fellowship. Now the scriptures do not divulge what went on during that time. I can only imagine that worship was happening when they met at the cool of the day [communicating one to one]. The Bible tells us that the angels' worship God, day in and day out and He made them. Then why wouldn't it be proper for Adam to do the same, since it was in the Garden, which was a miniature replica of Heaven. So now, let's use the keys that will open the treasure chest to the mystery of "One Flesh" and the keywords of life and blood. If we are going to understand the foundation of why these two words are essential to our subject of divorce, we must get a concrete contractual basis of God's view of "one flesh."

Genesis 2:18, 21-23, as we recall that God creates a woman, Eve. You can look at it as a surgery, however, we need to look at it as intimacy. Surprise? When God went into the man to create a woman, this was a private affair, as he was alone to bring forth another life. Here is the mystery. Only from man can life germinate. It is a scientific fact that without a man's DNA, the seed of a child cannot come forth. Let's go deeper. When a man is intimate with his wife and during the season of passion, he releases his fluids. In that fluid, called the sperm, is blood, which Leviticus tells us is life. When the woman conceives, it brings forth not just a child, the two become one and fulfills the commandment of God to replenish the earth. This also relates to 1Corinthians 7:2-5, where God allows a soul-tie to be created through the exchange of bodily fluids through the sperm, the carrier of the blood and the essence of life rather than the breath God breathed into man and he became a living soul. However, if there are any acts of fornication going on, then this brings forth death to a marriage.

When men follow the plan of God, this leads to obedience, and obedience leads individuals to keep His commandments, which in turn leads to truth, and truth leads to worship. So, a desire for a mate is not just our own but designed to lead us to a spiritual encounter with God beyond our average intellect or thinking. Who would believe that GOD telling them to replenish the earth would bring us into a full circle, to please the will of the almighty God? God's ways are not like ours, and there is no way we could figure out this on our own. The Father has to reveal this mystery. When couples realize that having only one mate for a lifetime puts them into total commitment and worship with God, their marriage can last forever. This causes us to examine how we handle marriage or even pause to think how our actions relates to GOD's initial purpose in the Garden is being fulfilled. Hence, marriages are being terminated daily by societal laws, ideas, and traditional norms. As you can see, governing from what has been happening down through the years is undoubtedly a rift from God's plan. If humanity continues to hold onto societal traditions and norms, there is no doubt that couples will not seek Godly ways to save their marriages.

No matter how we try to dress it up or down, the bottom line is, when God's plan for marriage was written, it was plain; there was no need to add or take away from what God initiated. It has become complicated from so many idealistic teachings and misunderstandings. Thereby, allowing the enemy's entrapment to continue to be a web of lies, anger, hurt, bitterness, and the list goes on – only looking for a way out, and that is through a divorce. Overall, no matter the outcome, we must do it God's way! Especially if we want to walk with Him and have our names called out before His Father.

"Give God your WEAKNESS and He'll give you, His STRENGTH."

– iBelieve.com

CHAPTER FIVE

Freedom

By now, I hope that the context of these pages has enlightened you or even given you a new understanding. If it has, then you or anyone else can no longer be bound by traditions or misinterpreted teachings concerning divorce. If anyone you know has been victimized by any contextual information and is enslaved to untold truth, you can now help them be free.

As we know, marriage is a commitment, and it will take work, not giving 50 – 50 but 100% from both the husband and the wife. Too often, couples enter their marriage thinking if they find someone they like and see some flaws here and there, they can fix them.

Well, let me let you in on a secret. YOU CAN'T! They

are not a project. You or I are not GOD to even try to do what only he can do. Leave the fixer-upper to the real estate industry. This type of attitude is the root of many divorces. No, marriage should never be entered into with the mindset that it is a merry-go-round where you can hop on or off when you want. Nor as a pair of shoes that can be exchanged when you don't like them any longer to be replaced with a new pair. Neither is it a game of checkers you play until it is over, and you get a new component. Husbands and wives should complement each other and not compete with one another. When the latter is being done, divorce is the result, and not one built on biblical principles but built upon ungodly self-motivated and selfish concepts.

How do we get there outside of counseling, prayer, fasting, and submitting to the will of God? Here is what I learned that would help couples to stay free. Become friends before you become lovers. This is key to a relationship. When you become lovers before you become friends, the relationship suffers because both the woman and the man may never come to the point of seeing the beauty of the person that they are dating. Look at it this way, almost everything in the marketplace comes with some sort of manual or instructions so that you can know how to utilize what you have purchased. Relationships are no different. How can couples enter a relationship with someone they don't know? One has no idea of their make up or their motives. No matter how many people you have encountered in your lifetime, every person is different, and you cannot treat each person the same. There is nothing identical in this world, not even identical twins. To our eyes, they look the same, but they are not. My mom was an identical twin, she and her sister looked the same, but they most certainly walked, talked, and behaved differently. Do as Proverbs 18:24 says, *"A man who has friends must himself be friendly, but there is a friend who sticks closer than a brother."* (NKJV) Strange as this sounds, if you take the time to examine your potential spouse and take it before God, it will prevent divorce later.

DO'S AND DON'TS

Don't marry for sex. I say again…DON'T MARRY JUST FOR SEX! You may be disappointed if they are not what you wanted, especially if you have been in previous relationships and engaged in premarital sex. You will find yourself constantly comparing them to the previous person that made you feel good, and this is a marriage killer within itself.

Don't marry just for money or what you can get out of the mate. Your future together should be on the grounds of how God wants you to replenish the earth, and these days it should be by way of ministry; someone needs your help.

Don't marry for looks, because as time goes on, those looks may change, not just because the person has aged; but a life challenge may surface. Then what are you going to do if they no longer look like the person you married? I have heard of cases where the mate got sick, and the wife or the husband left them. Sad, but true and certainly not what God wants. An instance where the marriage vows went out the window and a selfish spirit took its place.

Women don't look for a Boaz; let him find you! Instead, do what Queen Esther did. Prepare yourself. So, when he does come on the scene, you will be more prepared because you have spent time before God and are not acting out of desperation for a man. Through healing of past hurts, fasting, prayer, praise, and worship with God you will have a healthier relationship. Thereby giving the Holy Spirit free reign and permission to inform you when the man that God has prepared for you is seeking you. Be careful to follow GOD'S lead to ensure you don't end up with an undercover pimp, gigolo, or infidel. I challenge you to WAIT ON GOD, and don't let your flesh dictate your life partner.

Men don't go looking for a Brickhouse; she might be an undercover Delilah, Jezebel, cougar, or even a witch. Why do I say a Brickhouse? Because bricks are cold, dry, and complex. Yes, you want someone with a solid structural personality and good looks, but what about the holes inside the bricks that you don't see right away. Heed to the warning that was given to the women, WAIT ON GOD!

If you are divorced, don't remarry right away. Allow time for GOD to restore your mind, body, soul, and spirit. You will be no good to yourself or to the person that you start a new relationship with. Damaged goods, when utilized, often don't last long. Allow restoration to take place. Hurt people, hurt other people, and that is the best way to look at this advice. Un-enslave yourself, leave all your faults and fears at the Master's feet, as He works on you. Allow not only the fruit of the spirit to have its way but find comfort in knowing you will be free from the bondage of the past.

Don't justify your wrong or pain. Many marriages suffer when this happens. Look what happened in the Garden when the blame game was going on. It cost them greatly. God never intended for us to live in the yesterday, and when you do, one cannot move forward. There is a reward when you let go; trust me, I can truly testify of this for myself! When God confronted me with John 3:16 and 1 Peter 4:8 in this manner, He asked: *"Do you have my spirit?"* He asked me this three times, just like when He questioned Peter if he loved Him. My answer was yes, and then He hit me with this. *"My spirit is LOVE, and just as I covered you when you were in your sins, then why can't you cover someone else that has wronged you!"* I was speechless, my heart was shattered, and I wept tirelessly.

Husbands and wives, understand your roles. Men are responsible to LOVE according to Ephesians 5:25, 28, Colossians 3:19, and 1 Peter 3:7. If it is done correctly, as Christ loves the Church, the woman would not have a problem submitting as she should according to Ephesians 5:22 and Colossians 3:18. Wives don't be brawling women, constantly nagging and contentious. Wives when you learn the importance of and dynamics of submitting to your husband, you cause the atmosphere in your household to be a loving haven for your family to experience God's love, develop a personal relationship with God and spend all of eternity in Heaven with Him. I encourage every wife to practice Proverbs 31 daily.

Learn the love language of your mate. This will keep the fire burning for years to come.

Don't stop dating them and never get too comfortable thinking that you are okay; there is always room for improvement in your relationship.

In closing, I want to leave you with these two scriptures, John 8:36, *If the Son therefore shall make you free, ye shall be free indeed* and Romans 8:1, *There is therefore now no condemnation to them which are in Christ Jesus, who walk not after the flesh, but after the Spirit.* You now know the answer to the question of the century, Can I Divorce? And, the answer is yes, only for the grounds that have been revealed in God's word and not by traditions or what society has dictated to humanity. Stay free, and don't ever be deceived by the religiosity of Christendom. Let GOD be GOD and allow him to separate the wheat from the tariffs.

Father, in the Name of Jesus, I come lifting all those that may be found guilty of past sins and practices of religion in ignorance. I am asking for forgiveness and allow your spirit to lift the burden of those sins from the lives of those bound and who need to be free. I pray that the yoke of hurt, guilt, and pain be abolished and that your love will fill its void. Lord, help us to walk in the liberty as you have made us free by the shedding of your blood on Calvary's cross. Allow us to have a new mind, body, soul, and spirit not to hurt others or ourselves. Thank you for allowing me to share what you have given me over fifteen years ago so that others can be free as you have freed me. Thank you for loving us, and you didn't allow us to transition into eternity being in error. Let us now go forth and walk in truth and help others to embrace your word accordingly. In your mighty and matchless name, I ask that it be so, Lord Jesus Christ of Nazareth. AMEN.

"*Your PRAYERS don't have to be PERFECT; God hears your HEART.*"

– @therandomvibez

NOTES AND REFERENCES

CHAPTER 1

Michael Kuldiner – Michael Kuldiner, "History of Divorce, Origins, and Meaning." The Law Office of Michael Kuldiner, P.C., Attorney at Law, November 17, 2012. https://phillyesquire.com/history-of-divorce-meaning/. (Accessed 16 November 2020).

CHAPTER 3

Merriam-Webster. (n.d.). Incest. In Merriam-Webster.com dictionary. Retrieved May 30, 2021, from https://www.merriam-webster.com/dictionary/incest

"Orgy." Merriam-Webster.com Dictionary, Merriam-Webster, https://www.merriam-webster.com/dictionary/orgy. Accessed 22 Oct. 2021.

Dr. Carlina A. Wilkes

RECOMMENDED READING

The Right Way in Marriage for Women, by Cathy Rice (Murfreesboro, TN, Sword of the Lord Publishers, 1966). This book covers seven chapters on things women should be aware of in marriage.

Divorce the Wreck of Marriage, by John R. Rice (Murfreesboro, TN, Sword of the Lord Publishers, 1946). This book gives a literary Bible perspective of divorce and how to avoid it.

Dare to be a Man, by David G. Evans (New York, NY, Pilgrim Publishing Group, 2009). I highly recommend this book to every man and woman thinking about getting married or who has already been married. This work will help the reader to understand the opposite partner's personality.

Loose that Man and Let Him Go, by T.D. Jakes (Ada, MI, Baker Publishing Group, 1996). Another book is highly recommended for couples to glean more insight on the personality of a man's trait and his responsibility in walking as GOD has designed him to be.

The Power of a Praying Wife, by Stormie Omartian (Eugene, OR, Harvest House Publishers, 2014). This book is a must-have for every married woman. It teaches praying techniques for the husband, and mistakes to avoid that could lead to separation or divorce.

The Power of a Praying Husband, by Stormie Omartian (Eugene, OR, Harvest House Publishers, 2014). This influential book teaches a husband how to cover his wife and understand his position as her covering, prevent divorce and keep his happily ever after.

The Power of Prayer to Change Your Marriage, by Stormie Omartian (Eugene, OR, Harvest House Publishers, 2009). Woven in this prayer book are nuggets that will help couples stay close knitted to GOD and each other.

I thought it was My Mate, but it was Me Too, by Bishop Clifton Jones (Philadelphia, MS, A Voice Crying Ministries). The twenty-three chapters of this book answers questions about marriage and provides tips and tool on how to avoid the pitfall of divorce. This exceptional book is authored by a seasoned, established leader of the Pentecostal Assemblies of the World.

Fireproof, by Alex Kendrick, Stephen Kendrick, Eric Wilson (Nashville, TN: Thomas Nelson Publishers, 2008). More than a love story. It teaches how to save your marriage and recognize signs of divorce.

Love Dare, By Alex Kendrick, Stephen Kendrick, (Nashville, TN: Thomas Nelson Publishers, 2008). The companion book to Fireproof is a must-have, and it helps with self-counseling to prevent a divorce if done with the proper attitude and discipline.

The Divorce Recovery Guide: Get Your Life Back, by Josh David (North Charleston, SC, CreateSpace Independent Publishing Platform, 2014). A self-help tool for those who have divorced and are seeking to regain their focus on living again.

Live Again: Wholeness After Divorce 8 Sessions, by Michelle Borquez (Peabody, MA, Aspire Press, 2013). Many women and men feel helpless and unable to handle the downfall of divorce. Learn the author's 8 sessions to build: Acceptance, Forgiveness, Loneliness, The Real Enemy, Regain Self Respect, How to deal with Sexless and Single, How to deal with Shame and Guilt and lastly to discover the New You.

Dr. Carlina A. Wilkes

ABOUT THE AUTHOR

Dr. Carlina Annette (Hunt) Wilkes is the eldest of three children born during her parents' marriage, Carl Hunt and Mae Belle Lane. They divorced when she was about four years of age. She remembers living back and forth between both parents throughout her childhood but solely living with her father and stepmother. The spiritual foundation of that home began in the Baptist church, then continued in the Pentecostal Faith of the Church of GOD in Christ.

After graduating from High School in 1980, she entered the United States Army at seventeen [serving this country for thirteen years, two months, eight-day active duty, and three years as a reservist], when her life would change forever. No longer under her parent's rules and instructions, the author discovered that something was missing from her life.

In 1981, while stationed at her first duty station, Fort Carson, Colorado, she met her husband, Thomas Gene Wilkes, and on August 1, 1981, they became husband and wife and still united to this very day. Of this union, they have four children, eighteen grandchildren, and four Godchildren.

In 1983/1984, while stationed in Baumholder West Germany, GOD allowed her to befriend a couple, Brother and Sister Mitchell, who witnessed to her about the Name of Jesus. It was a wonderful experience, and she began her spiritual journey with GOD under the leadership of Pastor Tuttle of the United Pentecostal Church Ministry there in Baumholder, receiving the gift of the Holy Ghost and later baptized in the Name of Jesus for the remission of sin. The author's passion for the Word of GOD began as a student attending Sunday School, later becoming a Christian Education teacher, and continued from that point on. She has taught throughout her years in many venues where she fellowshipped as she traveled during her active- duty tour in the United States Army.

In 1992 before separating from active duty in 1993, she heeded her calling as a minister of the gospel. She further enhanced her knowledge outside that of the Bible, and in 1999 she made history. She was the first Afro-American of the South Bend Campus's first graduating class to receive her Bachelor's degree in Applied Management from Tri-State University, Angola, Indiana. In addition to graduating, she was also honored named on the the 1998- 1999 National Deans List. In, 2010 she continued her studies and received her Master's in Ministry from Indiana Wesleyan University, Marion, Indiana.

The author in 2011 received her ordination as an Evangelist with the Pentecostal Assemblies of the World, Inc.; after that, in 2016, she received her Certificate in

Accounting from Ivy Tech Community College, Indianapolis, Indiana. Finally, in 2020 she completed her education with the Doctorate in Ministry with Apostolic Theological Seminary, Inc., Kaplan, Louisiana.

The author also believes that GOD has given her a special gift to teach and preach GOD's Word to every generation, especially today's youth. On Friday, August 1, 2014, at 5:00 a.m. Central Standard Time on Blog Talk Radio, doors were opened for her teaching to be heard all over the world. Listeners of all ages could feast from her God-given ability, as she's sponsored by Prophet and Teacher Dr. Laron Matthews, Ph.D., Pastor of Restoration Foundation Prophetic International Ministers of Harvey, Illinois, with the blessings of her pastor Bishop Charles M. Finnell. You can tune into the live broadcast at: [www.blogtalkradio.com/prophetlaronmatthews]. This internet radio ministry is still going strong every first and third Friday at 5:00 a.m. Central Standard Time - For that, we give GOD the praise.

Today, the author continues in Ministry to help those looking for truth through GOD's word and helping those who live a holy life for GOD and be prosperous in the Kingdom of GOD. She also streams on Sunday mornings at 9:30 a.m. Eastern Standard Time from her Facebook page by teaching virtual Sunday School Classes.

Please feel free to join in on any virtual classes via her

personal Facebook page of Carlina A. Wilkes, Christ Temple Christian Sunday School Department, or her YouTube channel, Evangelist C. A. Wilkes. Lastly, to fulfill a 26-year calling of pastorship, Dr. Wilkes leads Chosen Generations Ministries and is the CEO/President of Center of Destiny, Inc., where she will be mentoring homeless, unwed, and abandoned mothers with their children.

Meet My Family Est. 1981

9 781957 551005